# THE ART OF TELLING A STORY

Myths and truths about famous writers' advice on how to write a novel

Baltazar Boeuf

# Table of Contents

# FOREWORD

If you're reading this book, it's because you probably read my _Creative Writing Workshop,_ a short manual with very specific techniques and tips for writing a novel.

However, the technique, the step by step is not everything when we learn a craft. A good part comes from your instinct and another from the inspiration of those who have walked this path before you.

Advice from famous writers are as useful as they are whimsical. They don't always suit everyone who is starting out in writing. Sometimes they tend to be contradictory or not entirely clear. This is because each writer develops his or her own process and along the way sticks with some rules and discards others.

There are tips that sound great but when we put them into practice, they turn out to be a burden, and there are tips that work for us at a given moment, but then not so much.

I have compiled here the advice of writers that I have followed or at least tried to follow, and I have commented on them according to my my experience as a writer and writing teacher. In some cases, I added some examples of how I think they can be used.

The famous writers quoted here are not just my favorites and belong to a wide variety of styles and genres. What has interested me most is their approach to the act of writing and how it has worked for some of my students while being disastrous for others. In the selection, I have discarded a lot of personal advice that, while useful, is more for life than for writing (run every morning, get married, get a dog, go out drinking, etc.).

My own remarks to this advice can be interpreted as advice in itself. It is in no way an attempt to modify the originals or to make a guideline. The aim of this book is for you, the reader, to form your own criteria when it comes to following these tips and make them part of your daily life as a writer, or simply to discard them.

To make the reading more enjoyable, I classified them in different topics about the act of writing: the use of sentences, the execution of drafts, the construction of characters, reading as a source of inspiration, the search for your own voice, the use of experience and imagination, the myth of the blank page, the audience of your stories and, of course, a section of anti-advice, that is, how to develop the criteria to follow some rules and break others (as many as necessary).

# THE SIMPLICITY OF THE COMPLEX

You may have grown tired of hearing the expression "less is more" to refer to a form of aesthetic attribute. It has become an empty advice after so much repetition. In fact, personally, I find the phrase "more is more" eloquent and easier to apply. In the field of literature, we could say: more images are more pleasurable reading experiences, more situations produce more elaborate characters, more pages offer us more pleasure, etc.

I like to think that "less is more" is a way of not complicating unnecessarily what we say. Unless we want to write a book where we experiment with language, it is always better to go straight to the point, using the materials (in this case the words of our language) that we have more at hand and that are more natural to us. Of course, this choice will vary according to our background, our expectations, and our personal preferences.

Reaching simplicity requires practice, patience, and art. There are sentences, and even whole stories, that are forceful for their brevity, for what they do not say. Remember the six-word story attributed to Hemingway: "For sale: baby shoes, never worn". In those refined, direct, and simple lines nothing is missing, nothing is left over, but what intensity and resonance they have. It takes a lot of mastery, contention and editing skills to get there.

*It's possible, in a poem or short story, to write about commonplace things and objects using commonplace but precise language, and to endow those things—a chair, a window curtain, a fork, a stone, a woman's earring—with immense, even startling power*

Raymond Carver



Carver, master of the short story, presents in a few strokes a very deep vision of the world. His sentences are short, his dialogue precise and to some extent rough. His prose is unadorned because he doesn't want to distract us from the core.

His advice can be misinterpreted to mean that we should write as simply as we speak. Nothing could be further from that. Prose and speech are practically two different languages.

It is not a matter of transferring what is spoken to what is written, but neither should we write in a way that wants to distance ourselves so much from what is spoken that we complicate it unnecessarily by using words that are not common or by referring to an object not by its name but by means of a truculent description.

Prose, i.e. written language, should be as clear as possible. When we are narrating, the words kiss, table, umbrella, rain, etc., should be named with that first name, in the natural way that comes to mind when we think of it, the name that is common to all speakers and with which the reader can identify.

*The beginner should avoid using adjectives, except those of colour, size and number. Use as few adverbs as possible.*

V.S. Naipaul



The advice of the British-Trinidadian Nobel laureate is quite straightforward. He recommends us to minimize the use of adjectives and adverbs in order to achieve concise writing. It is addressed especially to beginners because it is common for those who are new to writing to want to embellish their prose.

I think this advice is a bit exaggerated, especially regarding the use of adjectives. If we do the exercise of reviewing our own or someone else's text and eliminate all adjectives that are not of color, size and number, we will be left with a text with something missing. Adjectives such as fragile, dirty, bitter, soft are relevant as long as they are significant to the story. Many times, we can't just delete them. For example, if we say that a character drank from a glass of fragile crystal wine, the adjective is superfluous, but if we say that the relationship of two people became fragile after a certain event, the adjective does bring relevant meaning to the situation.

I find that a more useful way to approach this advice is not to adjectivize all nouns. In almost most cases they do not need this accompaniment, especially when they are obvious: red apple, hard wall, warm hug. In other cases, you should avoid very vague adjectives such as: **splendid** day, **wonderful** teacher, **unparalleled** experience. They don't really mean anything and in such cases, it is better to describe what makes such nouns wonderful, unparalleled or splendid.

The same is true of adverbs that modify verbs and adjectives. Not all verbs or adjectives need to be modified. Instead of qualifying actions and attributes with a vague adverb (he was driving **fast**, he told me **slowly**, she was a **bit** hungry), it is better to develop the situation or provide a more precise fact: he was driving at over a hundred miles per hour, he modulated every word precisely, she had not eaten for several hours and she was getting hungry.

*****

*I write as straight as I can, just as I walk as straight as I can, because that is the best way to get there.*

H.G. Wells

*****

Walking is an act determined by our genes and does not require exhaustive or specialized training, we can aspire to write as naturally as we walk. Everyone wants to write in a different way, but few want to walk in a particular way (unless we are gag actors or clowns). We just walk because we want to go from one place to another. We don't think of putting one foot in a particular way and bending the knee with a particular flair. That's what this advice from Wells refers to, we should move naturally so that the reader moves on the page with equal ease. So, when you write, think of yourself as simply walking and don't get in your own way, just move forward.

*****

*We should not force the reader to read a sentence twice.*

Gabriel García Márquez

*****

A sentence should only be read more than once for pleasure, or we like the way it sounds, or we want to come back to it to appreciate what it means, but if we have to read it again to understand it, it is because we are distracted, or it is written in such a convoluted way that it breaks with the story. When we are reading a narrative, we don't want to be taken out of it and a sentence with multiple incises and complements or words that don't fit well in the discourse are like a stone in the road. I refer here to fiction writing where the important thing is to tell a story. In poetry where the important things are images, rhythm and sound, there are other rules, just as in philosophical or scientific texts where elaborated concepts surely deserve to be read more than once. So, when you tell a story, do not put stones in the reader's path, unless you want him to stumble or look for another way, that is, another book.

Sometimes you may panic about the excessive repetition of words and use synonymy. As for the verb "to say" in dialogues, there are authors who replace it in a way that ends up being abusive and uncomfortable for the reader, who deep down knows that the author wanted to write "to say", but opted for a kind of make-up, for example: mumbled, referred, spat, babbled, uttered, expressed, declared, manifested, asserted, stated, formulated, enunciated, articulated, recited, etc. None of these verbs replaces the original action which is "said", in fact they misrepresent it and make it sound strange and unnatural.

This does not mean that every line of dialogue must be closed by a "said", but rather that many times the verb is not necessary, as it is usually clear who is speaking. If you feel you need to clarify who is talking, you can introduce some lines of dialogue with actions of the characters (example: Katy took a puff on her cigarette before answering, John looked at the painting behind her as she spoke to him).

In some cases, it is convenient to use in dialogues verbs such as: asked, answered, whispered, repeated, added... but not to replace "said", but to give strength to a certain line of dialogue in which a question is asked, an answer is given, something already said is reiterated or very important information is added to what has already been said. Other verbs that add nuances and can be used after a line of dialogue are begged, protested, scolded, ordered... because they give a clear intention to the words of the characters.

Regarding the second part of Elmore Leonard's advice, I suggest introducing some dialogues with situations where you describe what the characters feel or think, so you don't always have to write: "he said very slowly", "she said delicately", "she responded nervously", "he said severely". It would be more appropriate to create an atmosphere where these characters progressively experience the moods that accompany their speech.

Finally, I would like to emphasize that I don't think it's terrible if you occasionally use some verb of speech (referred, commented, expressed, etc.) to replace the verb "said" if it flows naturally, I mean, it's not forced. Every writer appropriates words and readers get used to the fact that certain writers use certain words constantly and organically.

*** 

*Always try to use the language so as to make quite clear what you mean and make sure your sentence couldn't mean anything else.*

C. S. Lewis

***

Avoid ambiguity, that is, write in such a way that a sentence does not have more than one meaning. Do not put the reader in the awkward situation of figuring out which meaning is the one you meant to express. Simplicity does not guarantee that a sentence has only one meaning.

Let's read these sentences and see if they have more than one meaning: "Vivian rode the horse with a crown". "The murderer killed the teacher with a book". Who was wearing the crown, Vivian, or the horse? Was the book a murder weapon or an object carried by the professor?

As you can see, although for the hypothetical author the answers to these questions are clear, the reader may have legitimate doubts that make him or her understand something different or stop to analyze the sentence to try to give it an unambiguous meaning.

*****

*Describe all with loving, quiet, humble sincerity,
and use, to express yourself, the things in your
environment, the images from your dreams, and
the objects of your memory.*

Rainer Maria Rilke

*****

Although this is very personal advice, we can draw
a lesson from its subjectivity. We can narrate
memories, dreams or imaginations as they are
presented to us, without any particular
embellishment. If we write them spontaneously,
the reader will be able to recreate them just as
naturally when reading them. If what we want to
tell represents something valuable, it is better to
write it in a crystalline, direct and concise way as
we feel it. Rhetoric usually kills emotion.

***

*Don't write anything that you wouldn't say out loud. Don't say "perhaps", say "maybe". Don't say "yet" when you mean "but". And so on.*

Lev Grossman

***

The advice does not refer to not writing bad words or ideas that you prefer to reserve for the private sphere, but to not use in writing those phrases that you do not use in our day to day.

In my opinion, it is not that certain words should not be used. There are tens of thousands of words in our language for a reason. If we condemned them to oblivion, they would disappear. I insist that this type of advice varies from author to author. If for you the expression "perhaps", "lineage", "nuptials" come naturally to you as part of your language and are constant in your text, I consider it is valid to use them.

Everyone takes advantage of the richness of language. Also, language is not the same for everyone because it depends on our tastes, our education, and our context. I only recommend that you use it with awareness and do not fall into the temptation of replacing " house" with " shelter" or "dwelling" just because you want to use a different word than the most common, or because you think you must use synonyms all the time.

# WRITING IS REWRITING

As we saw in the previous chapter, simplicity is not simple; refining a text to make it readable, pleasant and clear requires a lot of work. The beauty of simplicity does not just sprout, it requires multiple adjustments until we reach the sentence we consider appropriate.

There is no magic number of drafts or attempts, that is up to each author to decide according to his or her own preferences and expectations, but revisions and reworking are undoubtedly the most time-consuming part of the writing process.

Writing is not about going through long periods of reflection until that perfect sentence we are looking for comes naturally, but rather trial and error, multiple adjustments until we find the best possible way to present an idea, a dialogue, a description or a series of events.

Don't mix writing with rewriting. They are different processes that require different journeys, even different periods of time. If you write a page and that same day or the next you want to revise and redo it, you will make little progress or your progress will be so slow that frustration will prevail over patience.

Forget that there is such a thing as the perfect page. When you write, don't think about it, don't think about how you will correct it. Move on and only when you have made enough progress or are too exhausted to produce new material, then revise and rewrite. Move forward without pause as if that first draft were publishable material (even though it clearly is not). Accumulating pages, even if they are discardable, is much better than being stuck for weeks on a well-written page.

*** 

*Books aren't written – they're rewritten.*

Michael Crichton

***

Certainly, writing is rewriting, going back over what has been written to polish it, like the sculptor works the stone, over and over again. This quote is equivalent to saying that writing is easy, the hard part is rewriting, that is, correcting, giving final form. Five, seven, nine, eleven drafts... before the final version. Not to make you feel overwhelmed, but if you're only on the second version of your draft, you're nowhere near finished. So, keep rewriting.

If we want to be as accurate as possible with our craft, maybe we should call ourselves *rewriters* instead of writers.

*** 

*Write freely and as rapidly as possible and throw the whole thing on paper. Never correct or rewrite until the whole thing is down. Rewrite in process is usually found to be an excuse for not going on.*

John Steinbeck

***

The fact that we know we have to rewrite our original text over and over again should not be taken as an excuse to stop indefinitely on a sentence or a chapter. The key is to move forward and then organize the times to make adjustments, and after the adjustments organize the times to make deep corrections.

Your first idea may be good or not so good, but if you feel it belongs in your story, just put it into simple words. Later you can reformulate it if it seems too poor or imprecise. You can only work on what is already written, not on ideas in your head. So, write as it comes to you, the bulk of the work comes later.

***

*The first draft of everything is shit.*

Ernest Hemingway

***

Indeed it is. The first draft is not a finished manuscript, it's far from it, it's raw material, so don't pretend it's otherwise. The fifth draft of a story or novel may already be the final one. However, the first draft is just as important because that's where the germ of everything is. If we were to think of writing as a marathon, the first yards are covered in a very clumsy way, but these yards are the crucial ones to pave the way. So, don't get discouraged, but don't get complacent about your first couple of drafts either. I recommend that you take some time between each of them, a couple of weeks or even a month, to get the necessary distance to polish it. In the meantime, you can work on other projects.

***

*Don't sit down in the middle of the woods. If you're lost in the plot or blocked, retrace your steps to where you went wrong. Then take the other road. And/or change the person. Change the tense. Change the opening page.*

Margaret Atwood

***

Basically, this is what a writer's day-to-day life must be like. Redo, retrace your steps.

I insist: don't feel bad if you are stuck on pages you know are no good. Even the greatest writers feel the same way, and they have no problem confessing that this happens to them. There will be one or two gifted people who manage to produce a perfect page in one sitting, but that's not how it works for most of us. Writing requires a lot of patience and a great capacity to go back and know when it is time to take other paths.

*****

*Don't write under the influence of emotions. Let them die and then evoke them. If you are then able to bring them back to life as they were, you will have reached the halfway point of art.*

Horacio Quiroga

*****

This quote reminds me of an advice from Stephen King who recommends not to have a notepad to write down ideas. According to him, if the idea is really good and capable of obsessing you, it will remain in you and mature, and at some point, over the years, it will emerge with greater strength and clarity.

I think that sometimes emotion makes us think that an idea is really good. But I do not recommend omitting the writing of that initial emotion, the best thing is to put it in writing; the images in the head are not the same as the words on paper or on the screen. Ideas must be translated and transferred to a physical medium, even if we discard them later. It is always better to have the germ there, visible, fixed, to examine it later with cold eyes, when the initial emotion has passed.

I prefer to interpret this advice as not blindly trusting what we write under that first emotion. Mastering the literary art certainly consists in reviving that original emotion, but I see no problem in taking some notes as a starting point.

Just as many ideas that at first seem fabulous to us eventually turn out to be clumsy, it also happens that some seemingly dull idea that we write without much emphasis then grows like a snowball and becomes something fantastic. So always carry your notebook with you, you can burn it if when you review it later you are not convinced by anything you wrote down there.

***

*Keep the story in a trunk for a whole year and, after that time, read it again. Then you will see everything more clearly. Write a novel. Write it for a whole year. Then shorten it for half a year and then publish it.*

Anton Chekhov

***

Perhaps a year is too long to let a story mature. The important thing about this advice is that every text needs some time in which we take a distance and approach it as if it were not written by us. We must put ourselves in the shoes of an editor, a very critical one, when it comes to rewriting our text.

The Russian author also suggests that shortening it should take us half the time it took us to write it. This is not to be taken literally, as everyone will take more or less time. For many authors, the ratio could be the reverse: write a novel for six months and then spend twelve months cutting it down.

In any case, what I find interesting is that it refers to downsizing, not enlarging. In the cutting, in the elimination of excess material, lies a large part of an author's talent. J. R. R. Tolkien used to say that he cut up to three quarters or more of what he wrote. Not for nothing did the writer Truman Capote say that he believed more in scissors than in pencil.

Sometimes we don't want to waste anything, but over time we develop the maturity to recognize that this is the way it should be.

But what needs to be eliminated then? Start with redundant descriptions, commonplaces, unnecessary adjectives, dialogues that don't provide new information, scenes that don't push the characters to move... in short, everything that is a stone in the road, everything that would make you as a reader give up or skip pages.

# FOLLOW YOUR HERO

The three fundamental pillars of narrative are characters, plot and narrative universe.

Short stories, because of their compact nature, tend to give more importance to plot, that is, to a rapid unfolding of events that generally leave us with a sense of perplexity. In the novel, although the plot is crucial, the characters have more time to evolve. In a short story, the characters are almost always already evolved, like gods who were born walking and mature. In the novel, characters are expected to change little by little. As for the narrative universes, they also have more development in the novel than in a short story.

Of these three elements, it is the advice related to character development that I find most valuable. We usually start writing thinking about a series of actions set in a context (fantastic or real). That is why the biggest risk, or at least the most common, is that the characters become puppets that we place in predetermined places and situations.

As readers, we tend to remember the characters more than the details of their adventures. Places and events may surprise us a lot, but they do not produce empathy as do people, their contradictions, their fears, their desires and their defeats.

The personality of a character will always be more memorable than the eccentricity of an action or the fantasy of a universe. My general recommendation is that, in order to create more vivid stories, do not adapt the characters to the situation, but the situation to the characters.

***

*First, find out what your hero wants, then just follow him.*

Ray Bradbury

***

A character should surprise yourself as the author. If your character follows each of the actions you have planned beforehand, he or she may end up not being a very believable character.

The best characters are those who rebel against your writing plan. Only in this way do they develop their true personality, that which makes them unique. If you treat your character like a puppet, your reader will perceive him or her in the same way: stiff, unfeeling, unable to blink, hesitate or take risks.

Treat your characters like people you spy on, follow them everywhere they go, and after a while you learn to know how they think. Based on that then write how you think they would act based on who they are and what happens to them.

***

*Everyone is a potential murderer. In everyone there arises from time to time the wish to kill, though not the will to kill.*

Agatha Christie

***

While I find this worldview exaggerated, the value of this advice is that you should consider your characters capable of doing things they apparently wouldn't do.

Profiling characters for a novel project helps you determine some physical characteristics and personality traits. That's fine as a starting point. But when it comes to writing you should explore their darker passions. Find out what they are capable of doing even if it contradicts their personality traits. Consider your own darkest desires and thoughts, those that only surface in moments of sadness, hopelessness, anger, madness. Under that magnifying glass you must also consider each of your characters.

***

*When writing a novel a writer should create living people; people not characters. A character is a caricature.*

Ernest Hemingway

***

I don't entirely agree with this quote. I think that characters can be credible even if they are exaggerated: Don Quixote, Sherlock Holmes, Lisbeth Salander, Ignatius Reilly, Matilda are characters with quite extreme traits, and they are full of life, they exist as much or more than many of our acquaintances.

The most important thing, after all, is that characters are consistent with themselves. And that their actions and motivations are congruent with their personality, however eccentric it may be.

Hemingway also advises that characters should be ordinary people in unusual situations; however, the opposite is very valid: extravagant people in ordinary situations. Both approaches work. The important thing is that the characters seem real, that they feel, that they have desires, hopes and fears.

***

*Every character should want something, even if it
is only a glass of water*

Kurt Vonnegut

***

Every character in a story must have a purpose, a need or a desire. That is what drives him or her. If the character has no need or desire, there is no story. This need can be as complex as getting a throne, escaping the mafia, recovering a lost love or something as simple as seeing the sea, getting a job or drinking a glass of water.

The image of the glass of water is not merely symbolic (in fact, for a character in a caravan in the desert it can be a vital goal). We cannot forget that characters occasionally have the need to satisfy basic needs. In a story, they must eventually eat, sleep, yawn, go to the bathroom, etc. On their journey, all the characters want something big, but they also want small things; the former makes them heroic, the latter makes them human.

***

*In writing, you must kill all your darlings.*

William Faulkner

***

This is another of those pieces of advice that you should not follow to the letter, much less if your story does not take place during a war or a zombie hecatomb. It is true that death is part of the cycle of life and eventually people die. That doesn't mean that in a story arc you have to go that far. I prefer to read this advice as not becoming obsessed with a character to the point of spoiling them and miraculously saving them from situations of real danger. If it's his turn to die, let him die, if not let him live, but don't patronize him. Even Connan Doyle killed his character Sherlock Holmes... although later he had to resurrect him.

***



*Write characters who are both 'very small and very tenacious; at once very frail and very heroic'. Let them have contradictions.*

Virginia Woolf

***

Contrast is richness. Try to give your characters contrasting but complementary traits. A good character is one that moves forward in the story carrying those contradictory characteristics that make him or her unique. Try to create characters that are at the same time sullen and tender, kind and stingy, sad and euphoric, heroic and hesitant, pessimistic and altruistic... Thus, in many of their decisions the characters will put something of each of these traits and the results will be unexpected.

*** 

*Be a Sadist. No matter how sweet and innocent your leading characters, make awful things happen to them-in order that the reader may see what they are made of.*

Kurt Vonnegut

***

As we mentioned earlier, don't be lenient with your characters. The experience they have to go through must be very hard for them to reveal their deep personality. Homelessness, fights, illnesses, deaths, betrayals produce extreme reactions in which each character will act according to how he/she really is.

If nothing harsh happens to them, your characters will behave in a flat way, without differentiating themselves from each other. These extreme situations can be triggered by chance, by other characters or by themselves, but in all cases, they are experiences that make them sharper.

The personality of all of us is almost always tamed, protected by the armor of normality, of predictability, and only emerges with real strength when we lose that stability. The same thing happens to your characters.

# IT ALL STARTS WITH READING

Writing is an extension of reading. We write because we have read so much that we want to emulate that magic. We write because we want a story to exist that has not yet been written. We write because we want to shape an obsession, a fantasy, a nightmare... I'm sure there are many more reasons, as many as there are writers; the act of writing is always linked to the act of reading. We can imagine a chef who does not find pleasure in eating, or a soccer player who is bored watching matches, but it is inconceivable a writer who does not like to read and who does not find the time to do so.

Much of the learning of the writer's craft comes from abundant, varied and passionate reading. From academic training as a writer one can learn specific details, glimpse paths, but in reality, what forms a writer is reading, and the more varied the better: novels, poetry, essays, manuals, short stories, memoirs, diaries, chronicles. Everything is nourishing. And in the case of fiction writers, of course a lot of fiction from different cultures, periods, and genres, classic and contemporary, postmodernist, horror, romance, pirates, magicians, seamstresses, warriors, etc., the scope is as varied as the imagination. The important thing is that you find those readings pleasurable, inspiring and that it serves as a model for you.

***

*Read, read, read everything – trash, classics, good
and bad, and see how they do it. Just like a
carpenter who works as an apprentice and studies
the master. Read! You'll absorb it. Then write. If it
is good, you'll find out. If it's not, throw it out the
window.*

William Faulkner

***

I like the fact that a Nobel Prize does not make distinctions or promote only reading what is in the canon.

The classics are vital for our formation as writers, but so are commercial novels; everything that does not enter the library of the most severe critics is important material for a writer, because pleasure and learning can be found in everything. From so much reading we learn to know what to expect from a good book. We develop a taste that in turn becomes a tool.

And from bad books we learn what not to do. But what are the bad books? That is a personal discovery. I consider them to be those that only repeat common places, that don't resonate, that don't surprise us, that don't immerse us in the story, that are tedious to finish and that leave us with a feeling of having wasted time between their pages. If a book gives you that feeling not only abandon it but also analyze what made you run away from its pages. If the effect is the opposite, underline, take notes and reflect on what made it wonderful.

***

*I am always chilled and astonished by the would-be writers who ask me for advice and admit, quite blithely, that they 'don't have time to read.' This is like a guy starting up Mount Everest saying that he didn't have time to buy any rope or pitons*
Stephen King

***

Reading is not an additional activity to writing. It is an essential part that sustains it. It is not a source of inspiration or initial knowledge that is then dispensable. Even a doctor or an airline pilot can learn and then pursue his profession without further instruction (although at some point he will be left behind), but with reading it is different, for although we can read with a critical eye to learn from the masters and try to decipher their techniques, as writers we read above all because reading gives us a place in the world. Books read become part of our spirit and they shape our voice.

It is true that there may be days when we are so deep in a writing project that we hardly have time for anything else, and we may read a little less, but in general, over the course of a literary career, the truth is that to write well you have to spend more hours reading than writing.

*Let others boast of the pages they have written; I am proud of the pages I have read.*

Jorge Luis Borges



One of the most notable exponents of universal literature, always prone to jokes and fine ironies, recognizes that the happiness of reading is superior to that of writing. For Borges the library is the ideal world, and writing is a footnote, a commentary on the universe of works already written.

In his fictions Borges mixed with great intelligence the invention with the commentary, the fake book with the real one. For him, reading and writing do not seem like two different verbs but are part of the same act. In his work converge mysticism, detective stories, historical data, philosophical refutation, paradoxes of immortality, perplexity about mirrors, encyclopedic data, wandering in labyrinths... all of this set upon the backdrop of his varied readings.

Borges is the best example of how a good reader (the one who reads in abundance, the one who lives to read, the one who reads with a different look, the one who criticizes and reveres at the same time) becomes a good writer.

***

*Read history, historical fiction, biography. Read mystery novels, fantasy, science fiction, horror, mainstream, literary classics, erotica, adventure, satire. Every writer has something to teach you, for good or ill. (And yes, you can learn from bad books as well as good ones — what not to do).*

George R. R. Martin

***

Even if you decide to write in a very specific genre, your book only stands a chance of being remarkable if you draw from a wide and diverse range of sources. Crime novels, botany essays, and science fiction stories are more useful to a romance writer than romance novels themselves, because in the mix is the germ of a possible innovative outcome. Remember that there are no pure genres.

# YOUR VOICE: STYLE AND BEAUTY

There are many definitions and approaches to aesthetics. The forms of beauty are as varied as there are cultures and eyes. The beautiful is what is pleasing to the senses but also beauty is the disturbing, the rhythmic, the chaotic.

Although an aesthetic text can be expressed in simple sentences (as we saw previously), the pieces of advice discussed in this section are about rhetoric and constructing images. It is a selection of quotes that shed light on the personal poetics of some authors.

What is important for you as a writer is to be aware that with time you will find or refine your style (your way of writing) to create original books that have a signature, that is, that those who read them know that behind them there is a voice with its obsessions, peculiarities and personal twists in the use of language.

*Don't tell me the moon is shining; show me the glint of light on broken glass.*

Anton Chekov



You have probably heard this advice a lot of times. Although I consider it very useful, I don't agree that we should always apply it.

There is nothing wrong with direct descriptions. In any book by a respected author, I'm sure you'll find phrases like: it was pouring rain, it was hot, the moon was shining. However, using only basic descriptions can give a feeling of over simplicity. An author always seeks to present things in a different way, not only to appear original but also because we get bored of saying the same thing in the same way over and over again. Also, original images are more likely to stick in the reader's mind just because of their novelty. To create images, I suggest that you change the viewpoint of what you want to show, that is, the gaze, just as do the remarkable film directors who vary the perspective of the camera to show us scenes from innovative points of view.

As in Chekhov's example, if your gaze is on the moon it is natural to say that it is shining because that is what you want to emphasize, but if you look at the ground you will see its reflection in the broken glass, which also provides another sensation (a broken glass evokes a situation of recent violence that produced its breakage or of carelessness if the broken glass has been there for a long time). Try to apply this principle to replace other descriptions. For example, to say that someone was hot look at their beads of sweat on the back of their neck, the stains under their soaked armpits, their tongue dry from dehydration, the plants dry (if it is a long period of heat), the dogs sheltering in the shade, etc.

Remember that there's nothing wrong with telling it straight, but you'll give the reader a broader and deeper picture if you look for different perspectives. There are always new approaches, that's why language doesn't run out.

***

*I have the words already. What I am seeking is the perfect order of words in the sentence. You can see for yourself how many different ways they might be arranged.*

James Joyce

***

That is exactly what style is all about, ordering the words, which although they are the same for everyone, each author arranges them in a different way.

There are more elaborate or more direct styles. Don't worry if yours is one or the other, the important thing is that it comes naturally to you, that you feel it flows. I don't mean that your writing style is the first way the words come out, but that when it comes to rewriting and correcting, you choose an arrangement of words, a punctuation of sentences and a type of speech (tragic, comic, ironic, nostalgic, paranoid, etc.) There are authors of long sentences with many incises, others of shorter sentences. There are those who are very descriptive, dreamlike, fast-paced, full of images, others are musical, caustic, reflective. I would dare to say that there are as many styles as there are authors; although it is true that there are many writers whose prose is difficult to identify, even if we love their stories.

James Joyce was a style obsessive. In part, his style was based on parodying, recreating, and subverting the styles of his predecessors. His masterpiece, *Ulysses*, seems to have been written by a hundred hands, not only for its length but also for the variety of registers. In his untranslatable *Finnegans Wake*, Joyce dynamited the notion of style by inventing words and phrases that can only be understood in the context of his work. It is a borderline case of experimentation with language.

***

*Write drunk, edit sober.*

Ernest Hemingway

***

At first I had thought of commenting on this advice in the chapter on rewriting, but I think it is more appropriate here because of the idea that style is also the confluence of our dark side with our luminous side. If we want to take it literally, I must say that I don't agree at all with writing drunk, the times I tried it I fell asleep on the keyboard. I prefer to interpret this advice as letting all the monsters out and then taming them when editing.

***

*Always be a poet, even in prose.*

Charles Baudelaire

***

Although they are two different realms, good prose should be written with the same devotion with which a poet crafts his verses. The advice refers more to the care to think out sentences than to the search for rhythm and musicality (which poetry demands but prose can do without).

I prefer a thousand times a story written in a plain style, with short sentences and forceful actions, rather than an elaborate and ornate prose, but which does not tell anything interesting and whose characters and actions lack depth. In storytelling, the important thing is to tell, and that is why stories that stand the test of time endure bad translations and will always be relevant.

*All fine prose is based on the verbs carrying the sentences.*

F. Scott Fitzgerald



Fiction is primarily about movement. Whether slow or fast, linear, or circular, every reader of novels and short stories usually expects the story and characters to move forward (or backward, but to move).

There are plenty of stories in which little or nothing happens. Personally, they bore me to death. Perhaps in the past I was seduced by existentialist plots, but over time I have preferred to return to the roots, to the narrative that progresses. For a story to move forward it is convenient to put verbs above adjectives. That is, try to narrate actions instead of just describing emotional states. Of course, you have to describe in a novel, that gives depth, but in the balance there should be more movements than sensations.

*** 

*Be yourself; everyone else is already taken.*

Oscar Wilde

***

Sincerity sounds simple but at first it is the hardest thing to achieve. Don't try to be like other writers you admire or who are successful, but try to discover who you are and be like that model.

It is not a matter of forcing yourself to be original, nor of inventing a colorful personality, but of knowing what your obsessions are, your themes, what excites you, what makes you uneasy, what you care about.

Once you identify yourself and what you want to write, your writing will be more fluid, more necessary, more vital, and therefore unique.

***

*In writing. Don't use adjectives which merely tell us how you want us to feel about the thing you are describing. I mean, instead of telling us a thing was 'terrible', describe it so that we'll be terrified. Don't say it was 'delightful'; make us say 'delightful' when we've read the description.*

C. S. Lewis

***

Although this tip is very useful and probably the most useful when creating images and feelings for the reader, there are times when we can be direct and say that the food was delicious or that the news was terrible. Don't worry or feel frustrated if you use adjectives to describe an object, person or situation. The function of adjectives should not be underestimated and in many cases, they work better than a poor or clumsy setting. I advise a balance that doesn't get in the way of your pacing; for example, if you're in the middle of fast-paced action where there's a splendid meal, use that adjective, not an evocation of ambience that distracts or slows down the action.

Like many other tips, this one refers to the ideal of prose, but the ideal is not always what works best. You can test this by looking for aesthetically pleasing and effective texts where direct adjectivation has been used.

59

# MUSES, EXPERIENCE, AND IMAGINATION

Where does the flow of stories that a writer produces come from? Do muses and inspiration really exist?

I prefer to believe that the muses are nothing more than the mixture of will, curiosity, experience, and imagination.

Will is the strength, discipline, and determination to become a writer and write every day or almost every day. Curiosity is the constant desire to read avidly, investigate phenomena, historical facts, and be attentive to what is going on around us. Experience is what happens to us despite ourselves or by our own will, as well as the experience of all the previous readings that have enriched our life. And finally, imagination is the exercise of daydreaming to invent new worlds because the world we live in, with its rules and limitations is not enough.

These four elements are, to a greater or lesser extent, the source of literature. There is no magic source or fairy of inspiration, or in any case, as Pablo Picasso said, "Inspiration exists, but it has to find you working".

*You can't wait for inspiration; you have to go after it with a club.*

Jack London



We can't be passive and wait for ideas to come on their own. The club is the pencil or the keyboard, you must be sitting there writing, trying out material, discarding a lot until in that set of pieces that come and go you finally find the flow of the story you want to tell. As we have said before: although you have to think and ruminate a lot before writing, the best way to think is by writing.

*** 

*A little autobiography and a lot of imagination are best.*

Raymond Carver

***

For Carver, invention is crucial, and his best seasoning is experience.

The advice is quite obvious in its message, although I would still like to point out that autobiography does not necessarily refer to what we have lived, but also to what we have seen firsthand. Not all of us are fortunate, or suffer the tragedy, of having particularly striking lives.

Although everything that happens can become literature, sometimes the routine of going to an office, buying bread, paying the bills can frustrate us, especially if we do not want to write an existentialist book but a plot with vicissitudes, twists, and turns. There are neighbors, colleagues at school or work, even public figures in our environment to whom things do happen, and the fact of having witnessed or heard them, counts as part of our autobiography. Our environment is also part of our experiences, and from these, even if they are not ours, we can draw on them to spice up the portions that are pure invention.

*** 

*I always write in the morning. In the morning one's head is particularly fresh. The best thoughts most often come in the morning after waking while still in bed or during the walk.*

Lev Tolstoy

***

One practical aspect of how to be ready for when "the muses visit us" is to carefully select your routine. We don't always have the hours we want because other duties get in the way. From the hours you have available throughout the day choose the time and place where you can regularly sit down to write. Some people find it works before dawn or as soon as the sun rises, others at lunchtime, in the evening or in the early morning. Although it is valid to try other people's routines to see if they work for us, designing your own is the best, even if the routine consists of something as odd as using three hours a day at different times of the day. The point is to use time effectively and not let ourselves be won over by excuses or non-literary daily tasks, which there will always be.

*A writer, I think, is someone who pays attention to the world.*

Susan Sontag



This advice is a more elegant way of saying that inspiration is in the eyes. The world is largely the readings, and the way those books read resonate in the world around us.

But even if you're the kind of writer who relies primarily on reading experiences, every now and then it's good to look up, at least to give context to what you read and to feel like you belong somewhere, just as every now and then whales come up from the depths to the surface to breathe.

It is unlikely that an ascetic with no access to or interest in the outside world would read this guide. In any case, I find the advice valuable, especially since what is going on around us is often the germ of a valuable story, so it is not a good idea to miss it by being so self-absorbed.

***

*Literature is a guided and deliberate dream.*

Jorge Luis Borges

***

Someday dreaming will be considered the tenth or twelfth art. In dreams is encrypted the experience of life in its purest and most mysterious version. Art is an approach to that part of the psyche that is revealed when dreaming or creating. It is true that we do not always remember what we dream, but when we do, and when the dreams are very elaborate, the sensation is the same or greater than that of having read a good book (it is our own book, of course).

As writers we are somewhat like the directors of our conscious dreams; writing can be a form of daydreaming. Regardless of whether we are closer to fantasy or realism, what is on paper is something that does not belong to the world of the everyday. It is a creation of a nature similar to that of dreams or nightmares, only that there is someone directing behind the scenes. I suggest the exercise of writing a story as if it were someone else's dream. You will see how you feel freer, and perhaps an unexpected richness will emerge in your prose.

***

*Every plot, worth the name, must be elaborated to its dénouement before anything be attempted with the pen. It is only with the dénouement constantly in view that we can give a plot its indispensable air of consequence, or causation, by making the incidents, and especially the tone at all points, tend to the development of the intention.*

Edgar Allan Poe

***

I must confess that I never use this advice because I have never agreed with it.

Although I consider myself more of a "compass writer" than a "map writer," I believe that even the latter, despite all the planning, do not know exactly the end of what they write. At least, I refuse to believe it.

If you already know the ending of your story it will be somewhat forced to bring your characters to that moment without making their actions seem stiff. I think you can write intuiting or wishing for some kind of ending -just as we live- but without being certain that the outcome will be that one.

Personally, I would find it very tedious to write stories where I know the ending. Even living would lack excitement and meaning if we knew the day and circumstances of our death or other important future events. But it's a matter of approaches. I prefer to write stories from the middle, so inspiration moves in both directions, forward and backward.

***

*In the course of writing my first novel, I learned several things. First, that "inspiration" is a bad word that cheating authors use to appear intellectually respectable. As the old saying goes: genius is ten percent inspiration and ninety percent perspiration.*

Umberto Eco

***

This clever play on words has a lot of truth to it. To say that we have not been visited by the muses or that we do not feel inspired to write can become an eternal excuse. Paralysis is the opposite of creation, because creation is movement, trial and error, sweat and tears.

When you are asked why you haven't written anything new or why you haven't made progress on your current project and you think of answering that you *haven't been inspired*, you'd better bite your tongue and get to work.

*****

*A book must be the axe for the frozen sea inside us.*

Franz Kafka

*****

As a reader, you will receive the axe blow when you read a powerful book that touches your soul. As a writer, you must hit yourself in the chest. That is inspiration for Kafka, the crucial blow that undermines what we think we are to get to the bottom, to what we really are under the iceberg. Inspiration can also be obsession, desire, disturbance, loneliness, madness, despair... Look for your personal feeling that can be the equivalent for you, your own axe.

# OVERCOMING THE BLANK PAGE

The legendary terror of the blank page is the fear of not being able to write, of running out of ideas, inventiveness, and necessity. It doesn't happen to all writers, and many resolve it by getting down to work and filling the void with words. But for others it paralyzes them, and the paralysis can turn into trauma to the point of stopping writing for long periods.

For someone who has already written several books, it can be a consolation and stimulus to think that if the feat has been done before, it can be repeated, but when you are just starting out, there is no past to compare with and this can lead to a frustration that may take you away from the craft of writing.

It is normal that many times we get a little paralyzed, but we must make an effort to reverse that feeling so that it does not become a habit. In many professions, there is also the confrontation with the blank page with each new task, but architects, fashion designers, illustrators or doctors are not paralyzed by that ghost.

Although I understand that the emptiness of the page can intimidate you, write something, no matter if the sentence sounds poor or dispensable, this can help the page to contain something and the mythical fear vanishes. Let's see what some writers advise on this subject.

***

*Over twenty years I have probably averaged five hundred words a day for five days a week. I can produce a novel in a year, and that allows time for revision and the correction of the typescript.*

Graham Greene

***

Think small, I mean small amounts. If every time you sit down at the keyboard you have in mind everything you need to complete your thousand-page tetralogy by volume, you will feel as if you have to cross the continent on foot. The way to go is only a few miles per day. The same goes for the minimum two hundred, five hundred or one thousand words per day. There is no magic number in this regard, so set your own goals that are manageable and realistic for you.

My commentary to this advice is just over two hundred words long. Three times this length isn't really that much, so you can achieve it every day. And it doesn't even have to be every day, it can be every other day, or you can also rest on weekends, or you can even skip one day and the next meet your established quota.

Over time, these amounts will seem so little to you that you'll be able to write a lot more without even realizing it.

So, in short, don't think about the blank page but about the number of words you have set yourself to write without fail every working day. It is a matter of patience and perseverance so that all those empty pages will be filled little by little.

***

*Forget the books you want to write. Think only of the book you are writing.*

Henry Miller

***

Work and put your mind and heart on one book at a time, one chapter at a time, one scene or dialogue at a time. Focus your attention on that instant without looking forward or backward.

If you often feel paralyzed because you are thinking about another book to write and not the one you have in hand, then move on to that one, the point is not to get stuck. A work is built little by little; while painting, an artist is not thinking about the thousand paintings he will make in a lifetime, just as an engineer does not linger thinking about all the bridges he will build. The only certainty is the present, the work in progress, and that is why it is convenient to act accordingly. There is no harm if you take a note that has occurred to you for a different project while you are writing one, but you must return quickly to the one you are working on and accomplish what you have set as your objective that day.

***

*You can fix anything but a blank page.*

Nora Roberts

***

Repeat out loud this phrase every time you feel that the words do not sprout from your fingers.

Write as it comes out, do not meditate too much on the sentences before writing them because a good sentence is only achieved once it is on paper and you can correct it. As we mentioned in the rewriting chapter, the important thing is editing and proofreading; do not expect a first sentence to be perfect, not even acceptable. Don't worry about your first drafts even if they sound like the babbling of a child learning to speak. You can always edit, modify or discard it. It will be more natural for you to flow over something already written than something just thought out. We are writers because we put words on paper; if the letters are fluttering around in our heads we are just thinkers or mere dilettantes.

As an exercise, you can always write something even if you don't plan to use it in your book: a character's food, what he dreamed, a gift she received on her birthday, lines from a poem she read as a child, a fictional article from a newspaper where your story takes place, a random dialogue of your character in a grocery store... anything can move you forward.

*There is always, of course, that terrible three weeks, or a month which you have to get through when you are trying to get started on a book. There is no agony like it.*

Agatha Christie



If a prolific writer like Agatha Christie suffered the beginnings and then persevered, we can do the same.

The kick-off is like a race that starts on a very steep slope, we may feel that we are not moving in the first yards, but we have to keep going. Once we overcome this stage everything will flow better, either because we finish the project or because we decide to discard it to make way for another one.

I also think that it is not only the startup that is difficult. Sometimes we can be in the middle or even further along and suffer the agony of feeling that we are not able to continue. Think of the example of the race, and that this bump is just another hill in the middle of the road. You must continue in spite of eventual frustrations. All art is an exercise of will.

***

*If you write one short story a week, doesn't matter what the quality is to start, but at least you're practicing. And at the end of the year you have 52 short stories. And I defy you to write 52 bad ones. Can't be done.*

Ray Bradbury

***

Writing daily, or at least very consistently, is the only way to improve. "Quantity produces quality. If you only write a few things, you are doomed," the author of Fahrenheit 451 also said.

Take the advice as a challenge. When you carry it out, besides improving with practice, the blank page issue will not even bother you because your purpose will be clear: to write a story every week.

A weekly or daily story for a certain period of time will give you incredible agility and a lot of discipline.

Although all the tips compiled in this guide have a focus for the solitary author, at this point I invite you to do this writing challenge with some friends who are also starting out in the art of storytelling.

***

*When you have something to say, say it; when you don't, say it too. Always write.*

Augusto Monterroso

***

Don't wait until you have an idea to write it down. Most good ideas happen when you tell them or put them on paper, not before.

As we have said repeatedly in this book, you can only write by writing. Flannery O'Connor said, "I write because I don't know what I think until I read what I say. I write to discover what I know". Indeed, that process cannot occur before the words are on paper, because mental processes are vague until we ground them. It is such an obvious notion that we sometimes overlook it, and so we procrastinate the act of writing.

Have you written anything today, even one line? Monterroso is famous for having written several of the best hyper-brief stories, some as short as a few words.

***

*Abandon the idea that you are ever going to finish. Lose track of the 400 pages and write just one page for each day. It helps.*

John Steinbeck

***

If brevity is not your thing, but your aspiration is to be a full-length novelist, take it step by step, write one page at a time. One at a time you have a medium novel per year and three at a time a novel of great length. Of course, you have to consider editing, trimming, rewriting, but while you're in the first draft process don't think about that because it will be overwhelming.

It works for many writers, established or amateur, to keep track in a spreadsheet or notebook of the pages written per day. This serves as an encouragement when the number starts to grow. Personally, for books signed by me and for those I write under pen names, I prefer to keep a word count rather than a page count. Changing the font, size or line spacing may not give us a standard measurement in different projects, but character or word count is more accurate and all word processors have that tool. Whichever method

you choose, remember that you only have one day
at a time, it is a law of physics that no one escapes.

# YOUR IDEAL READER

Some writers' advice addresses the issue of the audience. Who am I writing for? What kind of reader will enjoy my text? Even if the answer to your motivation as a writer is that you are writing for yourself and no one else, if your goal is to publish and not burn your texts, then there is necessarily someone who will find your pages.

Many don't care who that supposed reader is, others are very clear about it. And although the image of the recipient should not influence us when we write, the truth is that sometimes we cannot help thinking about it.

Of course, there will be readers who will hate our writing, others who will make fun of it, get bored, underestimate it, but also -if our work is good- there will be readers who will enjoy it, underline passages, quote us and recommend us. Among these there will be those who will laugh, be frightened, be enthusiastic, be satisfied or expect to read more from us....

The ideal reader is the person who in our mind will be the one who values, understands and enjoys the book in the way we have planned. It is very difficult to find someone with all these characteristics and tastes. However, this abstract, almost phantasmagoric figure, guides the steps of many authors who think of a audience when they write.

85

***

*Write to please just one person. If you open a window and make love to the world, so to speak, your story will get pneumonia.*

Kurt Vonnegut

***

It is not wrong to write targeting someone in particular, or at least a specific type of reader. We write and publish to be liked, to please or annoy others. It doesn't matter that we sign with a pen name or that we are far from the publishing world; we always aspire that our readers enjoy, think, get inspired or suffer (in the cathartic sense of the term) with what we write.

But don't abuse it by wanting to write for many, because in the eagerness to please many, you will end up creating a hodgepodge. Vonnegut advises to write for only one person. I think you can be more permissive and choose a handful of readers -maybe three or five- for your work, as long as they are not so different in taste from each other.

In some of his advice, John Steinbeck also suggests that we should write for only one person, an acquaintance or an invented one. I'm more inclined to go with someone real, whether you know them in person or not. Someone real has a definite personality, if you invent a reader you can fall into the trap of accommodating them to force them to like what you write.

****

*Don't try to anticipate an 'ideal reader' – there may be one, but he/she is reading someone else.*

Joyce Carol Oates

****

There are authors who prefer to disregard the notion of the ideal reader. I prefer to rely on that compass even if it leads me to a different destination than expected. The ideal reader -even if he or she does not exist or is busy with another author- silently communicates his or her reactions to our text. Even those who write for themselves, to distill and translate their thoughts, the idea of that invisible reader is very useful to establish a sort of interaction and thus achieve a clearer text for us.

*If you really want to understand something, the best way is to try and explain it to someone else.*

Douglas Adams



This sentence is not exactly advice for writers but a line of dialogue from one of Adams' novels.

I like the idea that we write to understand certain obsessions, and that invisible receiver is a mirror who listens to us and is able to understand us when we arrange our words. To explain something to someone else is also to explain it to ourselves. Even if your work is more intimate literature, think of that ideal reader as a sort of confessor who must clearly understand your sins and obsessions in order to feel them as his own.

*****

*The public is the only critic whose judgment is worth anything at all.*

Mark Twain

*****

Many writers warn against the danger, or naiveté, of writing for critics or literature professors. They advise instead to write for the general public.

The relationship between writers and critics is not always fruitful; sometimes it can be very tense, even rough and poisonous. Anton Chekhov also agrees on this point: "Writing for critics makes as much sense as giving a cold person a sniff of flowers". This is not to belittle literary criticism, but in general we writers want passionate, enthusiastic, sincere readers. Criticism can sometimes be so cold that it neglects the pleasurable experience of reading, the aesthetic joy, the enjoyment of adventure.

Criticism or literary journalism are respectable professions, but they also have their own particular rules or even their own fashions. What the critics of one moment abhor, the critics of the next generation praise. A critic has specific motivations, but their opinions are not sacred

words. So, of all the ideal readers you may have in
your head I agree with Twain and Chekhov that
you should not write for the ephemeral applause
of the critic.

*** 

*An opening line should invite the reader to begin the story. It should say: Listen. Come in here. You want to know about this.*

Stephen King

***

There are tens of thousands of books waiting to be read. No one will read them all, it is impossible.
Many times, readers acquire a book by recommendation or because the author's name rings a bell, or because they liked the cover, or the title, but that does not mean that they will start reading it, much less that they will be satisfied until the final page.

If in the first sentence you give your readers a sentence that hooks them, that fills them with curiosity, that invites them to move on to the second sentence and from there to the third, and then to finish the chapter, you will have won them over in part. Writing is also about seduction, about creating the desire to want more.

***

If there's a book that you want to read, but it hasn't been written yet, then you must write it.

Toni Morrison

***

I believe that everything we want to read already exists, even if it is in another context, another epoch and another culture. It's a matter of knowing how to look for it. Personally, if I want to enjoy an innovative book, I prefer to discover it, not produce it.

I like to interpret this advice as the impulse to write something that escapes the mainstream and is not like everything else that is written in many genres.

There are a lot of readers waiting for just that: books that are risky, that don't follow trends, that turn stereotypes on their head, that renew narrative structures and points of view. That's the kind of reader you should think about when you write.

****

*When the writer gets bored writing, the reader gets bored reading.*

Gabriel García Márquez

****

Indeed, it is quite likely that your readers will experience some of the emotions that are the substratum of your writing. So as not to bore them, surprise yourself. So as not to disappoint them, deliver what is promised in your text. So as not to make them feel stupid, do not resolve situations with fortuitous outcomes. Always write with emotion and consideration, literature and art are a melting pot of our passions and emotions. If you write coldly or carelessly, the reader will read you like an iceberg.

***



*Do not think of your friends when you write, nor of the impression your story will make. Tell it as if your story were of no interest except to the small world of your characters, of whom you could have been one.*

Horacio Quiroga

***

For Quiroga it is not the readers who matter, but the characters; they are only interested in their story, not in who reads it, because they are living entities that are not there to please any reader.

But in our daily lives, do we, the characters of our story, live only for ourselves? Are not our fellow human beings, our gods, or our laws also a form of readers? It is really difficult to live and be in a vacuum, as if the gaze of others did not exist. I think that even in real live there are a couple of ideal readers whom we take into consideration for many of our actions.

***

*If you want to write for yourself, get a diary. If you want to write for your friends, get a blog. If you want to write for others ... become an author.*

James Patterson

***

A personal diary or a blog are written texts, but a literary author is one who aspires to reach the public in order to change their lives, not just to entertain or provide useful information.

As narrative authors our purpose is to tell unforgettable stories that intrigue readers, that move them, disturb them, make them think, change the world or make them forget it momentarily while they are immersed in our pages. Since Scheherazade and her many stories told during a thousand and one nights (to save herself and many women from the fury of the murderous Sultan Shahriar) that has been the mission of authors: to tell in order to save, not always life, but to save from tedium, from simplicity or from the everyday absurdity.

Even if you write in simple words or your stories are about ordinary themes, always keep in mind that a true author leaves a lasting

impression on his readers. That's what literature
is all about.

# BEND THE RULES

To conclude, I leave you some advice about the importance of breaking the rules and not following trends or advice. These quotes have no comments as they are self-explanatory. They are advice where the authors are exhorted to create their own path and discard other people's experiences.

Except for perseverance and enthusiasm for reading, there are really no formulas and each writer faces the personal challenge of making his or her experience unique. There are no rules for a book to be wonderful, for if there were, it would be very easy to produce a great book every time, and if that were the case, literature would lose its charm. So, you can break all the rules and ignore all the advice and still manage to write a good book.

*****

*There are three rules for writing a novel.
Unfortunately, no one knows what they are.*

Somerset Maugham

*****

*This is how you do it: you sit down at the
keyboard and you put one word after another until
it's done. It's that easy, and that hard.*

Neil Gaiman

*****

*Ignore all proffered rules and create your own,
suitable for what you want to say.*

Michael Moorcock

*** 

*A writer is someone who has taught his mind to misbehave.*

Oscar Wilde

***

*If someone gives you a piece of advice that sounds right and feels right, use it. If someone gives you a piece of advice that sounds right and feels wrong, don't waste so much as a single second on it. It may be fine for someone else, but not for you.*

Etgar Keret

***

***

## AUTHOR'S NOTE

If you found this book useful or think it could be a guide for other readers, I would greatly appreciate it if you could leave me a **rating** and a brief **review** on the product purchase page. That detail, and sharing your reading on social networks, are the best rewards for any author. Thank you.

***

LET'S STAY IN TOUCH

If you would like to write to me, learn about my other books, read first chapters of works in progress or receive notifications of new releases or workshops, please subscribe here.

I don't send more than one email a month, sometimes not even that.

## About the author

Baltazar Boeuf (Valletta, 1971). Writer, translator, and photocopier guy. Author of *The Half Room*, *The Rebel Right*, *New Philosophy of Pain* and *Summer Camp*. Founding member of Babel Project. He has lived in the cities of Mérida, Caracas, Madrid, Mexico City, Portland.

* * *

I did an experiment: I took all the suggestions I wrote for this manual and turned them around. The result was a novel of absurd humor titled **The Half Room**. If you would like to read it, here is the link.